D0521054

Flying for Adventure

AMELIA EARHART

by *Mary Dodson Wade*

A Gateway Biography
The Millbrook Press
Brookfield, Connecticut

*For Tillie, who learned to fly
before she learned to drive.*

Cover photograph courtesy of The Bettmann Archive
Background cover photograph courtesy of Superstock

Photographs courtesy of: Smithsonian Institution: pp. 4 (photo
no. 78–16945), 32 (photo no. 80–11040); The Schlesinger Library,
Radcliffe College: pp. 7 (both), 11, 14; The New York Public
Library, Astor, Lenox, and Tilden Foundations: pp. 19, 43 (top);
Seaver Center for Western History Research, Natural History
Museum of Los Angeles County: pp. 22, 29; The Ninety-Nines:
p. 25; UPI/Bettmann: pp. 26, 38 (top); Reprinted with permission
of the Purdue University Libraries, Special Collections, West
Lafayette, Ind.: p. 35; AP/Wide World: pp. 38 (bottom), 43 (bottom).

Library of Congress Cataloging-in-Publication Data

Wade, Mary Dodson.
Amelia Earhart : flying for adventure / by Mary Dodson Wade.

p. cm. — (A Gateway biography)
Includes bibliographical references and index.
Summary: A biography of the famous woman pilot who set many
records before she was mysteriously lost over the Pacific Ocean
in 1937, emphasizing her belief that women could and should do
anything they set their minds to.
ISBN 0-395-64539-5 (pbk.)
1. Earhart, Amelia, 1897–1937—Juvenile literature. 2. Air
pilots—United States—Biography—Juvenile literature.
[1. Earhart, Amelia, 1897–1937. 2. Air pilots.] I. Title.
II. Series.
TL540.E3W33   1992
629.13′092—dc20
[B]   91–37645   CIP   AC

Amelia Earhart

*Amelia Earhart in
her leather flying outfit.*

Eleven-year-old *Amelia* followed her father around the Iowa State Fair. Sideshow barkers called out to fair-goers to see amazing wonders. Carnival rides whirled. Amelia put down fifteen cents and bought a hat made out of a peach basket.

At the edge of the fairground, a crowd gathered to look at a strange new machine—an airplane. Most people in 1908 had never ridden in an automobile. Yet there, behind the fence, was a machine that went up in the air. "Look, dear, it flies!" said one of the adults.

It was just wood, rusty wire, and canvas to Amelia. She went back to playing with her new hat. Before many years, however, the name of Amelia Earhart would be forever linked with airplanes.

She set record after record—altitude records, speed records, the first woman to fly alone across the Atlantic and Pacific oceans, the first person to make a round-trip coast-to-coast flight alone. She had nearly finished one more record-setting flight—circling the earth at the equator—when her plane was lost.

Amelia Earhart lived her life following her

dream, and she encouraged everyone, especially women, to do the same.

*A*melia Mary Earhart had been born at her grandparents' house in Atchison, Kansas, on July 24, 1897.

Grandfather Alfred Otis, a lawyer, had brought his bride to this booming town on the Missouri River. At his big house on a bluff overlooking the river, there were crystal chandeliers, gardens, and a wonderful library.

Amy, Amelia's mother, was the Otis's oldest child. Judge Otis had objected when Amy married Edwin Earhart. He felt Edwin could not support a family. Amelia's father was brilliant, charming, and well educated, but he never did earn much money. Amy had returned home when it was time for Amelia to be born, and the little girl was named for both her grandmothers.

Edwin was a lawyer for the railroad. He traveled often, and his wife went with him. When they were little, Amelia and her younger sister Muriel spent most of the time in Atchison.

This picture of Amy and Edwin Earhart, Amelia's parents, was taken in 1895.

Amelia at age six. Even when she was a little girl, she loved adventure and exploring.

Cousins next door joined them in picnics and mud battles. They explored caves along the river bluffs, but their greatest adventures took place in the barn. In a game they called Bogie, they took hair-raising make-believe journeys in an old carriage. Whipping imaginary horses, they careened wildly along, barely escaping snarling wolves. Suddenly, someone would yell, "WHAT'S THAT OVER THERE?" Everyone would shriek in terror at what might be hiding in the dark corner of the barn.

The Earharts and their cousins went to a private school. Amelia was a good student, but Grandmother Otis was horrified when she did things like jumping the fence in front of the house. "When I was a little girl," Grandmother Otis said, "I didn't do anything more strenuous than roll my hoop in the town square."

Amy Earhart, however, encouraged her girls to be independent. She even let them play in wide-leg bloomers while all the other girls wore ankle-length skirts.

It was a relief to everyone when Amelia learned to read. She curled up for hours in the big library. Reading became a habit. She and Muriel worked out a plan to make chores go faster. One of them read aloud while the other did the work.

Letters kept the girls in touch with their parents. "Dear Parallelepipedon" began one letter. Amelia scurried to the dictionary. She was sure her father knew every word in it. He may have. He went to college when he was fourteen.

One Christmas Amelia wrote:

Dear Dad,

Muriel and I would like footballs this year, please. We already have plenty of baseballs and bats.

To Amelia's surprise, along with the footballs, there was a small shotgun. Muriel had sent another letter without telling her.

Amelia also insisted on a boy's sled. It was no fun to ride sitting up in a girl's sled. One snowy day, she flopped down on her sled just as the junk man's cart came out of a side street. Amelia couldn't stop or turn. In a split second, she swooshed underneath the horse without a scratch. "If I had been sitting up," she said, "either my head or the horse's ribs would have suffered—probably the horse's ribs."

The girls rode bicycles and played baseball, basketball, hockey, and tennis. Their father taught them to fish.

More than anything, Amelia wanted a horse, but her pleas to fill the empty stall in the barn went unanswered. The horse next door was too tall to climb on, but when a delivery horse stopped in front of the house, Amelia used the shafts of the wagon to scramble up. It was a moment of heaven! Then someone had to come get her down. She also tried to ride a pony at her grandparents' summer vacation place in Minnesota. He munched the cookies she brought and then headed for low limbs to scrape her off his back.

When Amelia was ten, her family moved to Des Moines, Iowa. With Mr. Earhart's new job, the family sometimes traveled with him in a railroad car.

On Saturdays, Mr. Earhart entertained the neighborhood children with marvelous stories that turned into games in the barn behind the Earharts'

Amelia and her family sometimes traveled by train with their father. In this picture, Amelia (left) poses with her sister, Muriel, Mr. Earhart, and the family's Japanese cook, Tokimo.

house. Once, he got a scar on his nose when some-one slammed the hayloft door shut just as he poked his head up.

The children brought Saturday lunch and cooked on a homemade brick oven. Amelia experi-mented with unusual things. She used lots of flour and sugar trying to make manna, the food men-tioned in the Bible. She was sure it was small white muffins that tasted like angel food cake.

Happy times for the family soon ended, how-ever. Mr. Earhart began to drink heavily. He lost one job after another. They moved often. Perhaps because of her father, Amelia never used alcohol.

In spite of problems at home, the girls were good students. Muriel loved literature. Amelia de-voured chemistry and physics but exasperated her math teachers because she wouldn't explain how she got her answers.

She grew tall and thin. Because she was shy, boys didn't pay much attention to her. When Ame-lia graduated from Hyde Park High School in Chi-cago, the words under her yearbook picture said, "The girl in brown who walks alone." But her friends knew she was smart and funny.

After high school, she attended Ogontz College, near Philadelphia. Amelia wrote home about lessons and sports. She drew a picture of herself in the school uniform. "I look like a broomstick wrapped round and round," she said. Amelia was happy there, but she never finished college.

World War I was raging in Europe. Muriel had entered college in Toronto, Canada. During Amelia's senior year, she spent the Christmas holidays there with her sister and mother.

One day, she saw four soldiers helping each other walk. Each had lost a leg. "I want to stay here and work in the hospital," Amelia told her mother.

Ten hours a day she scrubbed floors, gave out medicine, and even played tennis with some patients. Amelia Earhart never forgot the horrors she saw. She always spoke against war.

For fun, she went to a nearby field and watched pilots take off and land. One day, she and a friend went to an air show. After many loops and rolls, the pilot grew bored and flew directly at the crowd.

Everyone in his path scattered. Her friend fled, but Amelia stood still. One part of her said, "RUN!" But the other part of her wanted to be in that

During World War I, Amelia worked as a volunteer nurse in a hospital for wounded soldiers in Toronto, Canada.

plane. Years later, Amelia told everyone, "That little red plane spoke to me as it swished by."

Amelia's *dream of flying* seemed impossible. Only the army trained pilots.

Soon the war ended, and Muriel entered college in Massachusetts. Amelia, who was recovering from an illness, joined her. She passed the time picking out tunes on an old guitar and also took a course in automobile engine repair.

Before long, Amelia went to New York City to study medicine. Students were not supposed to go into the tunnels underneath the buildings at Columbia University, but Amelia explored them all. She also climbed to the top of the library dome. Later, she led friends there to watch an eclipse of the sun. Soon, however, Amelia discovered that she didn't want to be a doctor.

By this time, her parents had separated, but Mr. Earhart wanted his family to come back. They joined him in California.

Amelia couldn't forget about airplanes, and one day her father took her to an air show. She sent him to ask one of the pilots about flying. Lessons cost a thousand dollars, but Amelia had made up her mind that she was going up. Three days later, her father paid a dollar for her first ride.

The plane took off. Miles away the Pacific Ocean spread out. Amelia was barely off the ground, but she knew she had to fly.

That night, she said casually, "I think I'd like to learn to fly." No one said anything.

Then she announced, "I signed up for lessons."

Her father stiffened. "You aren't serious! I can't afford that." Mr. Earhart thought if he didn't pay for the lessons, she wouldn't take them.

Amelia got a job working at the telephone office. She learned photography and earned a lot of money for a picture of an oil well gusher. She even drove a truck.

When she had money, she flew. For her lessons, she made the long walk to the airfield from the end of the trolley line. At first, she showed up wearing a silk blouse, riding pants, and laced boots.

One day, she wore an expensive leather jacket. "Dude!" said the mechanics. The next day the jacket was grease-stained and wrinkled. She had smeared oil on it and then slept in it. Because grease and dirt were everywhere, Amelia began to wear old army clothes like the other pilots. And she began cutting her long, blond hair a little at a time. Later, her tousled short hair became a trademark.

Anita Snook, one of the first women to get a pilot's license, was her teacher. Anita recognized Amelia's natural flying ability but felt her pupil took too many chances.

After nearly a year, it came time to solo. Amelia climbed almost a mile high, did a few maneuvers, and then made a very rough landing. "Were you scared?" asked one pilot.

Amelia didn't think she had done anything unusual.

The pilots teased her. "You were supposed to be scared. You didn't do anything right but land rottenly!"

For Amelia's twenty-fourth birthday, her mother and sister helped her buy a plane. She painted the Kinner Airster bright yellow and called it "The Canary." The small motor vibrated so much that

Amelia's feet went to sleep, but the little plane was all hers. Several weeks later, Amelia flew higher than any woman had before. The record was soon broken, but it was her first.

Even though Mr. Earhart had conquered his drinking problem, Amelia's parents divorced. Amelia sold "The Canary" and bought a car—a big yellow Kissel convertible. In "The Yellow Peril," with its wire wheels and spare tires in front of the passenger doors, she and her mother drove to Boston to join Muriel.

She kept touch with flying, but she worked at Denison House in a poor section of the city. She enjoyed directing activities for immigrant children who came there to learn American ways. She visited their homes and piled them into "The Yellow Peril" for rides.

One day, the telephone rang at Denison House. It was for Amelia. "Tell them I'm too busy to talk right now," she said.

"But he says it's important," replied the youngster who came to get her.

Amelia was annoyed as she walked to the phone. Then she heard Captain H. H. Railey say,

*Children from Denison House, where Amelia worked,
pile onto her car, which she called "The Yellow Peril."*

"Would you be interested in doing something for aviation? . . . It could be dangerous."

Amelia snapped to attention. Just a few months before, the world had gone crazy when a pilot named Charles Lindbergh flew alone across the Atlantic. What could Captain Railey want?

At their meeting that evening he asked, "Would you fly the Atlantic?"

It didn't take Amelia long to answer—"Yes."

She met the rest of the committee in New York City and learned that they were looking for a woman pilot to join two men on a flight across the Atlantic. Amelia's calm, intelligent answers met the qualifications set by Mrs. Amy Phipps Guest, who was paying for the trip.

Preparations were kept secret because others were planning the same thing. Amelia didn't go near the field as the *Friendship* was painted bright orange and fitted with pontoons. Extra fuel tanks replaced the seats.

At last, the *Friendship* was ready. They took off for Newfoundland. There, the crew anxiously waited two weeks for fog to clear. Finally, on June 18, 1928, Amelia crouched at a little table behind the pilot as the wheels left the runway. She punched the stopwatch and began to record the flight.

Amelia had a way of mixing beautiful thoughts with mangled English. During the flight she wrote, "There is nothing to see but churned mist, very white in the afternoon sun. . . . I have et a orange."

Amelia was flight captain, but she did not have a license for instrument flying. Because of fog, Bill Stultz stayed at the controls.

Twenty hours and forty minutes after they had taken off, they set down on the water near a little town in Wales, in Great Britain. At first nobody paid attention. Amelia waved a white towel out the front window. A man on shore took off his shirt and waved back. Finally, someone came to get them.

When they reached Southampton, England, they were mobbed by cheering crowds. "The girl in brown" never walked alone again.

The aviators went to teas and sporting matches. Three trunks of clothes arrived after people found out that Amelia had brought only a toothbrush. She visited Lady Mary Heath, a pilot, and bought her little plane.

Amelia (wearing her pilot's cap) surrounded by an admiring crowd at Southampton, England, having made her first trip across the Atlantic as flight captain.

All the praise made Amelia uncomfortable. She had not done any of the flying. President Calvin Coolidge sent congratulations, but she wired back, "Success entirely due to skill of Mr. Stultz." It pleased her greatly when Lady Nancy Astor, who was interested in settlement houses, wanted to talk about Amelia's work at Denison House.

Reporters, however, were happy with the new heroine. She was tall and slim and had tousled hair. With looks and manners like famous Charles Lindbergh's, Amelia quickly became known as Lady Lindy.

George Palmer Putnam had been on the committee that chose Amelia to fly the Atlantic. His family published books, and he was always on the lookout for things people would be interested in. He suggested that Amelia write a book. He also arranged speaking engagements for her and taught her how to talk before audiences. "Get rid of your hats," he said. "They are a menace!"

After she finished her first book, *20 Hrs. 40 Min.*, Amelia took off in the little plane she had bought in England. She saw friends at the National Air Exhibition in California. The 381st Aero Squadron made her an honorary major, and she proudly wore the pilot's silver wings they gave her.

After visiting her father, she flew back to New York. That made her the first person to fly a coast-to-coast round trip alone. She spoke to groups about the safety of air travel. She wrote for *Cosmopolitan* magazine and modeled for *Vanity Fair.*

When two friends started an air service between New York, Philadelphia, and Washington, Amelia took care of passenger problems. On one flight they flew with a pony standing in the aisle. They put goggles on him and took a picture.

On another, a woman who didn't want to pay for a second seat said she would hold her small dog. The dog turned out to be huge. Amelia noted, "The passenger sat *under* the dog."

In 1929, Amelia bought a Lockheed Vega. She flew it in the first Women's Air Derby. Will Rogers, the humorist, called the race a "Powder Puff Derby." Amelia was annoyed, but later they became friends. Her plane finished third, but Amelia felt that the race helped establish women as pilots.

Amelia (fourth from right) with other contestants
in the first Women's Air Derby, held in 1929.

In 1931 Amelia married George Putnam. This picture was taken at their home shortly after their wedding.

She pushed for an organization of women pilots, the Ninety-Nines, and was elected its first president. She dedicated her second book, *The Fun of It,* to them.

Even with a busy schedule of flying, she spent time with her dying father. Using money she earned from her books, lectures, and products that carried her name, she paid her father's debts. She regularly sent money to her mother, who lived with Muriel.

There were many good women pilots, but Amelia Earhart became the best known. The man responsible was handsome, energetic George Putnam.

George was divorced. Six times he asked Amelia to marry him. Finally, she said yes. But she felt George must know that she intended to keep flying. On their wedding day in 1931, Amelia handed George a letter:

There are some things which should be written before we are married. You know I hesitate because I am afraid I'll lose the chance to do things which mean so much to me. Let us not interfere with each other's work or play. Promise to let me go if we are not happy, but I will try to do my best in every way.   AE

Soon *after their marriage,* Amelia began flying an autogiro, a machine that was half-airplane, half-helicopter. She set an altitude record in it. This novelty plane was good for advertising. When Amelia flew one cross-country with "Beech-Nut" painted on the side, George's son passed out giant three-foot packets of gum.

When she was not flying, Amelia enjoyed their big house in Rye, New York. But George knew it bothered her that she had not really piloted an airplane across the Atlantic. He was not surprised one morning when she said, "Would you mind if I flew the Atlantic?"

George quickly set things in motion. Secretly, a new motor was put in Amelia's red Vega and extra gasoline tanks were added.

One day, just as Amelia got to the field, the hangar phone rang. "AE," called George excitedly,

The autogiro, a machine described as half-airplane, half-helicopter, offered Amelia a new challenge. She is pictured here after setting the altitude record for autogiros in 1931.

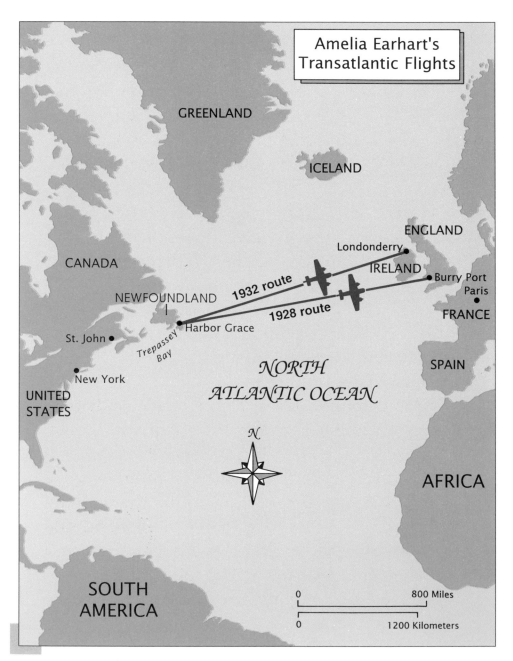

Amelia Earhart's Transatlantic Flights

GREENLAND

ICELAND

ENGLAND

CANADA

Londonderry

IRELAND

NEWFOUNDLAND

1932 route

Burry Port

Paris

Harbor Grace

1928 route

FRANCE

St. John

Trepassey Bay

New York

NORTH ATLANTIC OCEAN

SPAIN

UNITED STATES

N

AFRICA

SOUTH AMERICA

0   800 Miles

0   1200 Kilometers

"weather over the Atlantic is right if you take off now."

Forgetting about lunch, she rushed home, changed to jodhpurs, and grabbed her leather jacket and flying suit. A mechanic flew the plane to Newfoundland while Amelia slept before the long flight.

At 7:12 P.M. on May 20, 1932, Amelia was on her way alone across the Atlantic. It wasn't long before the hands on the altimeter began to spin uselessly. She could not tell how high she was.

Four hours later, ice formed on her windshield. To clear it, she went into a dive and pulled out so low that she could see the waves breaking. She climbed into fog.

Sipping tomato juice, she flew on. Suddenly, tongues of flame began shooting out of one engine. She watched anxiously, but it kept running.

Soon after daylight, she saw the green farms of Ireland. She had been flying more than fifteen hours when she set the Vega down in a field outside Londonderry. Workers nearby thought she was a man when they saw her flying suit.

Soon she was sipping tea at a nearby cottage

Amelia poses on her Vega in Londonderry, Ireland, having completed her first solo transatlantic flight in 1932.

while the world went wild. Exactly five years to the day after Charles Lindbergh made his solo flight across the Atlantic, a woman had done the same thing.

Lindbergh wired his congratulations. But the funniest message came from her dry cleaner. "Knew you would do it," he said. "I never lose a customer."

To people who asked why she would do such a thing, Amelia answered, "I wanted to. It proved to me, and to everyone else, that a woman with adequate experience could do it."

Amelia flew to England, where she was a celebrity. George joined her. In France, Amelia received the French Legion of Honor medal. She attended air races and laid wreaths at tombs. She met kings and queens. Still, she modestly insisted, "Special credit goes to the mechanic who prepared my plane. And I hope that transatlantic travel will become commonplace."

After sailing home on an ocean liner, Amelia received the Distinguished Medal of Honor from Congress. The National Geographic Society presented her with its Special Gold Medal, the first one given to a woman. Endless speaking engagements kept her busy. Famous people filled the house in Rye, New York.

As she continued to fly, Amelia broke women's speed records on transcontinental flights. She became the first woman to fly nonstop across the country. When the 1932 Olympic Games came to Los Angeles, she made sure she was there with her husband and stepson.

In October of that year, she was named Outstanding American Woman. In her acceptance speech, she recalled a glowing article about her in a French newspaper. It had ended by asking, "But can she bake a cake?" She accepted the award, she said, for all the cake bakers.

President Franklin Roosevelt and his wife invited Amelia and George to visit. Eleanor Roosevelt wanted to see Washington from the air, and the two women, dressed in evening clothes, flew over the city.

Besides flying and speaking, Amelia began designing clothes. She also had a line of luggage.

Soon she set her next goal—to fly across the Pacific Ocean alone. Nobody had done that before.

*Amelia and First Lady Eleanor Roosevelt
view Washington, D.C., from the air.*

"I'll take off from Hawaii," she told George. "A continent is harder to miss than an island." On January 11, 1935, the Vega nosed into the air at the Honolulu airport. The next morning, people surrounded her plane as it touched down in Oakland, California.

Purdue University invited the famous pilot to be a part-time professor. Amelia liked this school where women took engineering courses. She believed women had the right to tinker with motors, lathes, and jigsaws and to peer inside engines.

At the university, young women dropped by her room for long talks. The tall, skinny, thirty-eight-year-old legend sat on the floor with them, giving straightforward answers to their questions. In a questionnaire, she asked what courses would help them in a career. "If you are the first *woman* to want a particular career, what difference does it make? Try it. It might turn out to be fun. To me, having fun is a necessary part of work."

Amelia was almost forty years old and still having fun at her work. She had a new plane, a Lockheed

Electra. It was all metal with two motors and re-tractable landing gear. A friend, pilot Paul Mantz, took out the seats and filled the plane with every new gadget.

Amelia, who loved fast planes and sporty cars, had one more "first" to accomplish—to circle the globe at the equator. George pored over the maps with her. Then he went to Washington to get permission from all the countries she would fly over. He arranged for gasoline and spare parts to be at each stop.

With Fred Noonan as navigator, she made the first hop to Hawaii, but the plane was damaged taking off there and had to return to the mainland for repair. Two months later, Amelia and Fred were in Miami, Florida. Because of storms, they would fly east instead of west.

At 5:56 A.M. on June 1, 1937, George waved Amelia off on her last "stunt." Along the way, she kept notes she planned to turn into a book.

First they flew south to Venezuela and along the northeastern coast of South America. They crossed the Atlantic to the west coast of Africa before stopping in Ethiopia. They skirted the Ara-

Amelia in the cockpit of a new plane in 1937.

With navigator Fred Noonan, Amelia studies a map as they plan the route of her 1937 round-the-world flight.

bian peninsula because they could not get permission to cross, then landed in Karachi (in what is now Pakistan). There newspapers reported that they had been quarantined for yellow fever. Actually, each time they landed, attendants came on board to fumigate the plane. From Karachi, they flew across India and landed in Calcutta.

In Rangoon, Burma, they encountered the heavy rains of the monsoon. They flew on to Thailand, then Singapore. After stopping in Indonesia, they touched the northern edge of Australia.

In Lae, New Guinea, the people called little planes "insects" and larger ones "birds." To them, her plane looked like the tins English cookies came in. They called Amelia's Electra "biscuit box."

The night before the flight from Lae to Howland Island, Amelia Earhart wrote, "A month ago I was on the other side of the Pacific. Almost the whole width of the world has passed beneath us. Only this broad ocean is left. I will be glad when we have crossed it."

Just a few days before, Amelia and George had talked on the telephone. George asked, "Having a good time?"

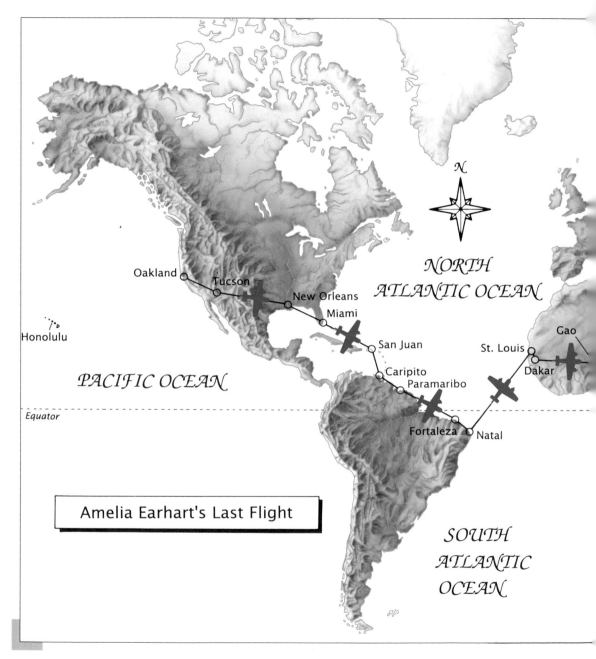

Amelia Earhart's Last Flight

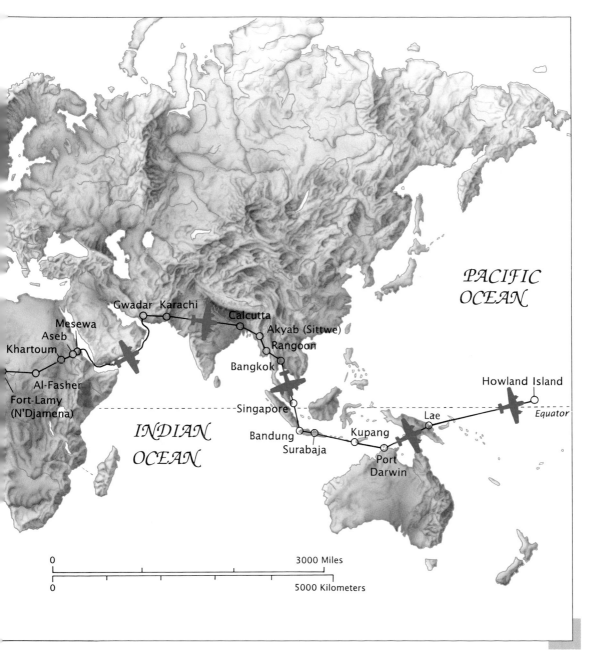

PACIFIC
OCEAN

Gwadar Karachi
Calcutta
Akyab (Sittwe)
Mesewa   Rangoon
Aseb
Khartoum   Bangkok
                                                                    Howland Island
Al-Fasher
Fort-Lamy   Singapore   Equator
(N'Djamena)   Lae
INDIAN   Bandung
OCEAN   Surabaja   Kupang
                                          Port
                                          Darwin

0   3000 Miles

0   5000 Kilometers

"You betcha!" came the answer. "It's a grand trip. We'll do it together sometime."

"OK with me," said George.

"I'll cable estimated time to Howland. See you in Oakland," she said.

Tiny Howland Island—½ mile (less than 1 kilometer) wide and only twice that long—was 2,500 miles (4,000 kilometers) away in the middle of the Pacific Ocean. Amelia never reached it.

The Electra took off from Lae on July 2, 1937. The ship *Itasca* waited near Howland to guide her. Fourteen hours after Amelia left Lae, radio operators on the *Itasca* heard her say "cloudy and overcast." The *Itasca* constantly transmitted messages to her, and black smoke streamed from the ship's smokestacks to help guide her.

Five more hours went by. Amelia's voice came in stronger, "We must be over you but cannot see you. Gas is running low."

Amelia called for information. The *Itasca* kept listening and transmitting, but Amelia's radio equipment could not pick up the signal. Only once did she say that she heard them. They never got her position.

These words, written by Amelia to her husband before she left, reveal her courage.

> Please know I am quite aware of the hazards. I want to do it because I want to do it. Women must try to do things as men have tried. When they fail, their failure must be but a challenge to others.

Amelia waves good-bye from her plane before leaving on what was to be her last flight.

Nearly twenty hours after she took off, Amelia Earhart spoke hurriedly, "We're running north and south." Those were the last words anyone heard her say.

A massive search started, but she was not found. Over the years, many people tried to learn what happened. World War II began soon afterward, and rumors started that Amelia was on a spy mission and had been captured by the Japanese. But evidence suggests that she ran out of fuel and crashed into the ocean. In 1992, searchers found what they said was debris from her plane on a deserted island far south of Howland. But the evidence was unclear, and the mystery remained.

Amelia Earhart planned this flight as her last big one. She knew the danger, and she left letters for her family to open if she did not return. Her letter to George said:

Please know I am quite aware of the hazards. I want to do it because I want to do it. Women must try to do things as men have tried. When they fail, their failure must be but a challenge to others.

Important Dates

1897 Amelia Mary Earhart born in Atchison, Kansas, on July 24.

1916 Graduated from Hyde Park High School, Chicago.

1918 Nurse for veterans in Toronto, Canada.

1919 Entered Columbia University for medical training.

1920 Went to California with parents; first ride in a plane.

1921 Flying lessons with Anita Snook; soloed.

1922 Set first flying record, for altitude (14,000 feet, or 4,270 meters).

1926 Social worker at Denison House, Boston.

1928 Flew Atlantic; wrote *20 Hrs. 40 Min.*; flew first solo round-trip transcontinental flight.

1929 Many speaking tours; bought Lockheed Vega; took part in first Women's Air Derby.

1930 Organized Ninety-Nines.

1931 Married George Putnam; flew autogiro to altitude record.

1932 Wrote *The Fun of It;* flew Atlantic solo.

1933 Visited Roosevelts at the White House; took part in National Air Races; broke transcontinental records.

1935 Flew first solo flight from Hawaii to U.S. mainland.

1937 Lost while on round-the-world flight July 2; *Last Flight*, edited by George Putnam, published.

Further Reading

Amelia Earhart, Aviation Pioneer, by Roxanne Chadwick (Lerner, 1987).

By the Seat of Their Pants, by Phil Ault (Dodd, Mead, 1978).

Flight: A Panorama of Aviation, by Melvin B. Zisfein (Knopf, 1981).

Lost Star: The Story of Amelia Earhart, by Patricia Lauber (Scholastic, 1988).

Plane Talk: Aviators' and Astronauts' Own Stories, edited by Oliver Carl (Houghton Mifflin, 1980).

Whatever Happened to Amelia Earhart? by Melinda Blau (Raintree, 1983).

By Amelia Earhart

20 Hrs. 40 Min. (Putnam, 1928).

The Fun of It (Harcourt Brace, 1932).

Last Flight, edited by George Putnam (Harcourt Brace, 1937).

Index